Dedicated to our patients and their families who have given us the privilege of being guests in their lives at some of their most challenging and vulnerable moments.

To Steve + Mary Darlington

Ed Eckstein
3/20/10

Bricks&Mortals

a hospital observed

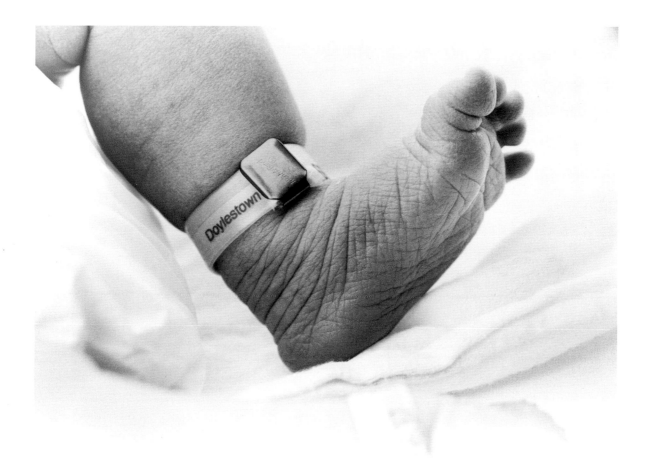

photographs by
Ed Eckstein

Printed in China by Global PSD
Published by Ecksray Press

ISBN: 978-0-615-19803-3

book and jacket design: Michelle Boehm

The mission of Doylestown Hospital is to provide a responsive, healing environment for our patients and their families, and to improve the quality of life for all members of our community.

I recall the fear on my friends' faces when I first told them that I was going to spend most of a summer at Doylestown Hospital. When they asked me about the procedure I was going in for, I told them it was creative loitering. But as I would find out, the real procedure was open heart—the heart that is extended to everyone who comes through the hospital doors, from the administration down to the people in the snack bar who made my appropriately enough, black and white shakes.

The medical images that we thrill to in films and on television often stray far from the real face of healthcare. *Day after day I found the smallest, most routine moments to be the most moving.* At a time when hospitals draw increasing criticism for being impersonal, mechanical and unfeeling, I was continuously impressed by the compassion of the caregivers and the valor of the patients I was privileged to photograph.

My intent was first to capture an honest and accurate record of medical moments, but second and even more important, a journal of moments that capture what is universal about the ways we take care of each other.

Ed Eckstein

photographer

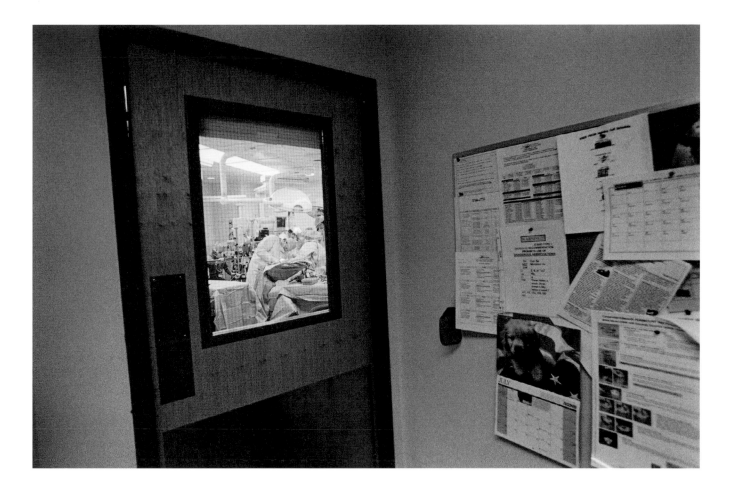

Work is love made visible. *Khalil Gibran*

If you could stand in the center of our hospital and magically peer through the walls, what would you see? Gleaming treatment rooms, imposing machines and miles of tubes, pipes and wires. Hundreds of people focused on tasks they have learned to perform with skill and precision. Mountains of papers and rooms full of charts; mobile computers, trays of instruments and giant cameras. You would see groups of caregivers huddled in conversation, and anxious patients waiting for news that will either ease their pain or confirm their fears.

Would you see love? Absolutely and undeniably.

Every person who has chosen health care as his or her life's work senses, at a very personal level, the truth behind Gibran's words. Beyond the myriad details of life within a hospital, beneath the vital signs, staffing ratios and Medicare codes, these are the reasons that call us here—a need to connect, to make things better, to alleviate suffering, to bring comfort, to promote healing.

The photos contained in this book confirm that love is both visible and at work—comforting, healing and transforming the lives of the people who work at Doylestown Hospital, and the patients we serve. Each picture captures a moment in time and reveals a story from two perspectives; those who are cared for and those who provide care. Our fondest wish is that these photographs allow patients to glimpse into the hearts of their caregivers, and help each member of our hospital family recall the spirit of purpose and love that called them to their profession.

Richard A. Reif
President | CEO
Doylestown Hospital

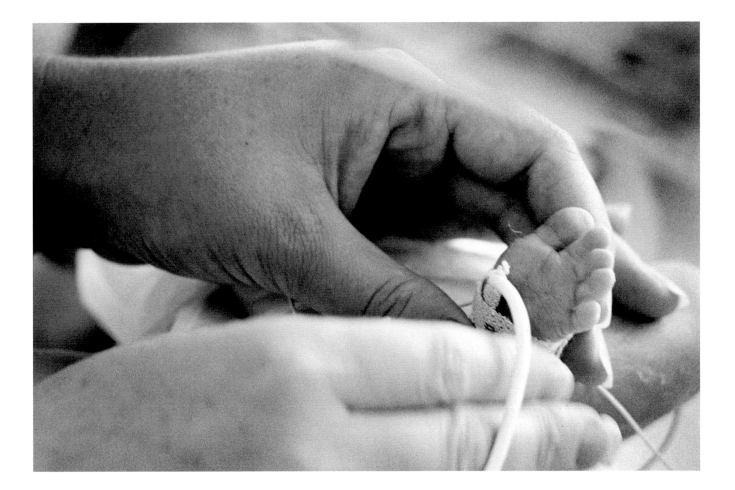

Every job is a self-portrait of the person who does it.
Autograph your work with excellence.

Anonymous

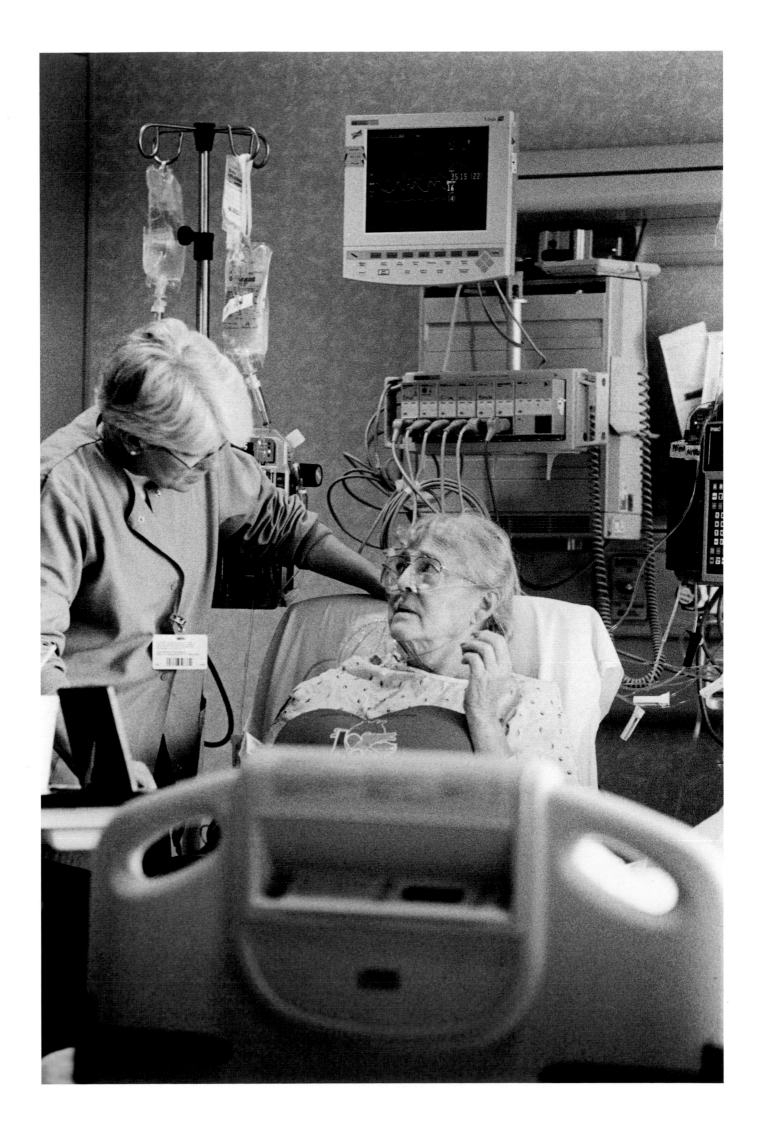

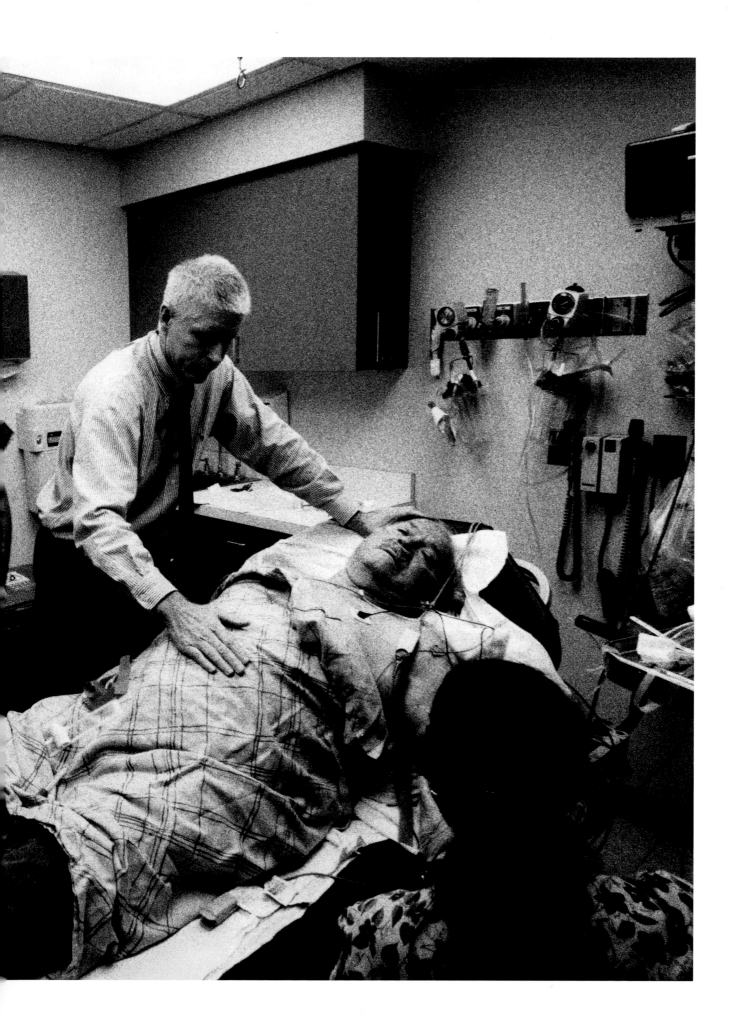

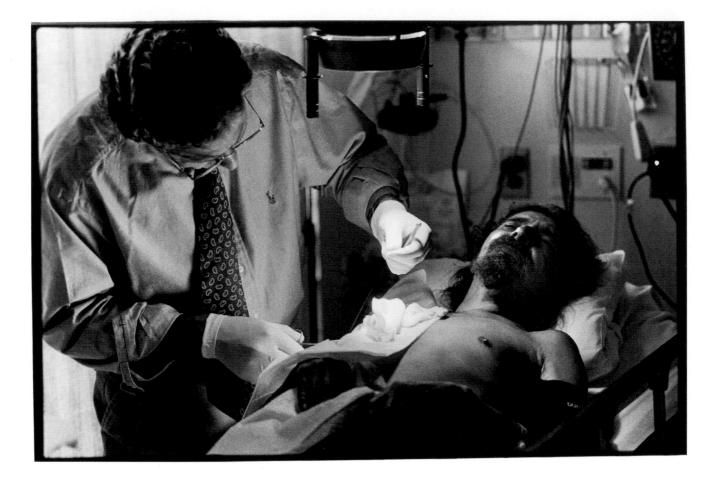

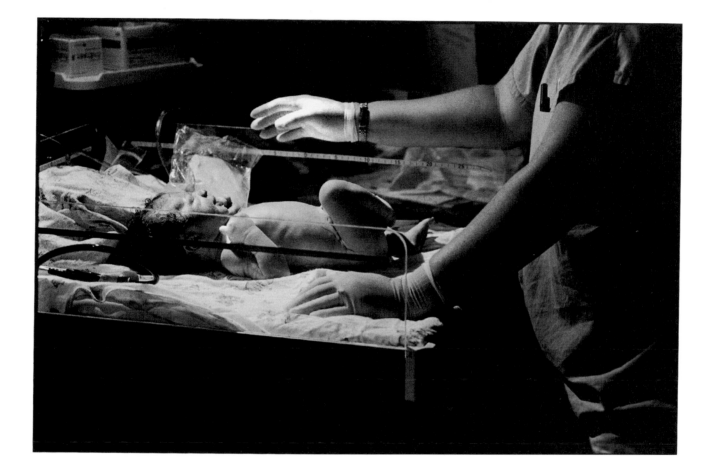

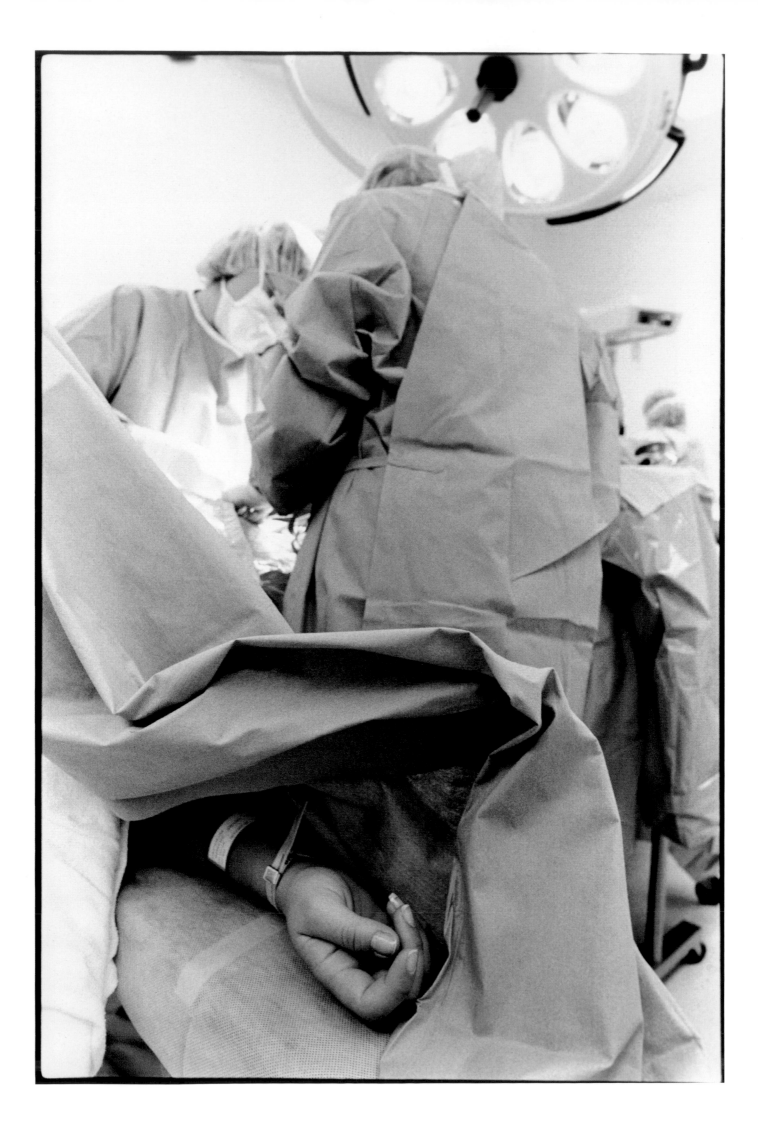

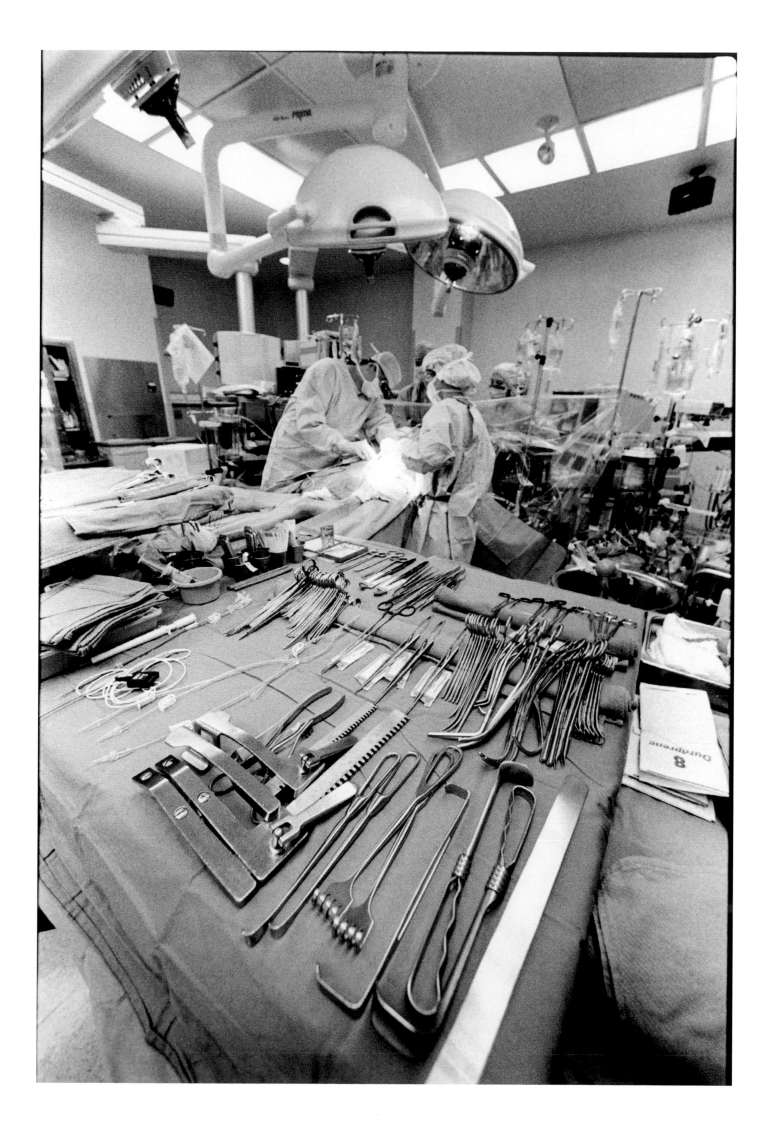

Compassion brings us to a stop, and for a moment we rise above ourselves.

Mason Cooley

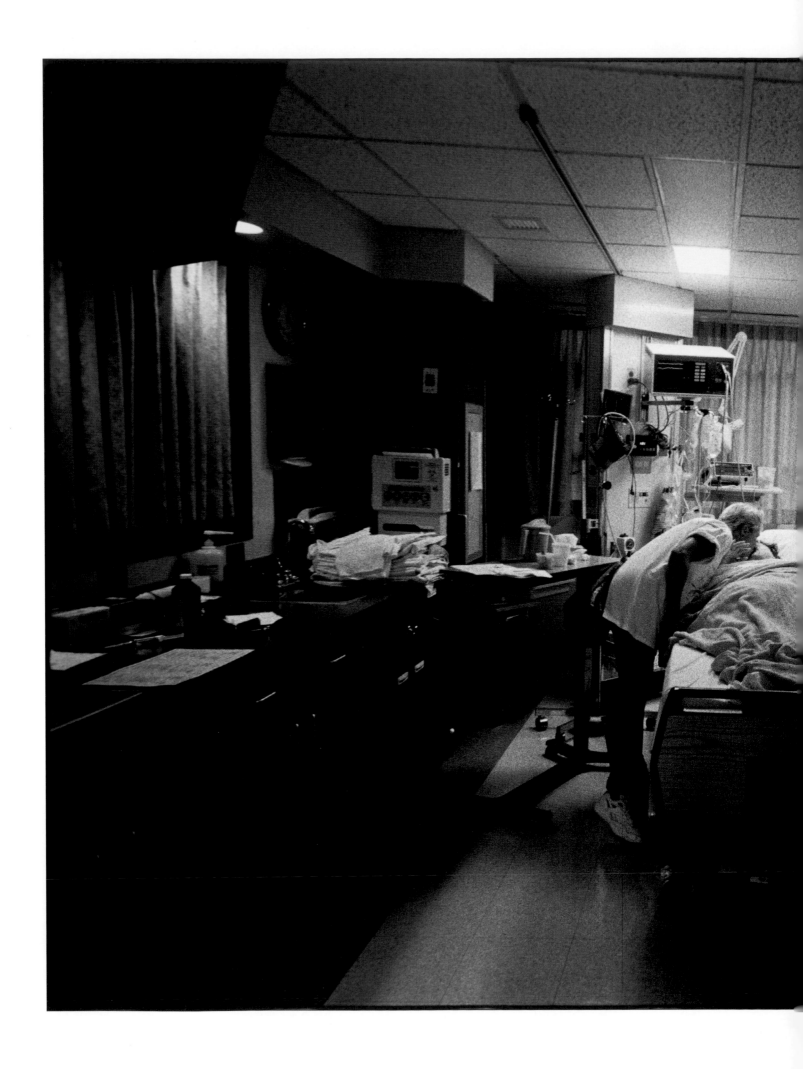

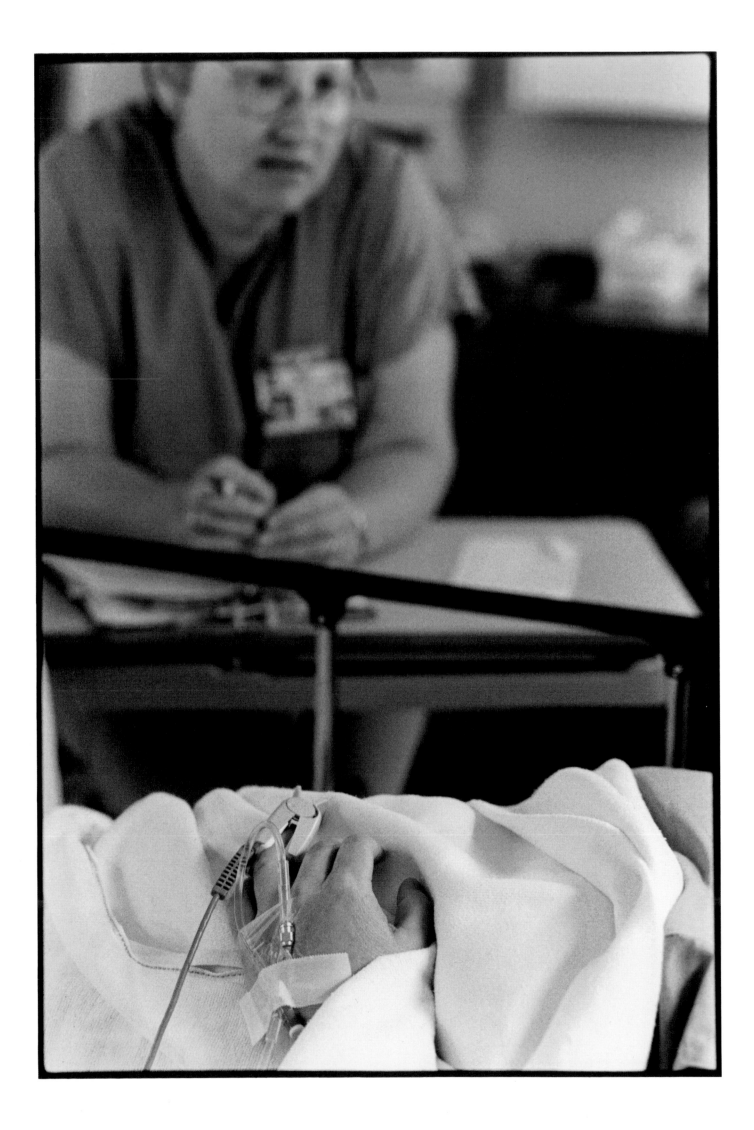

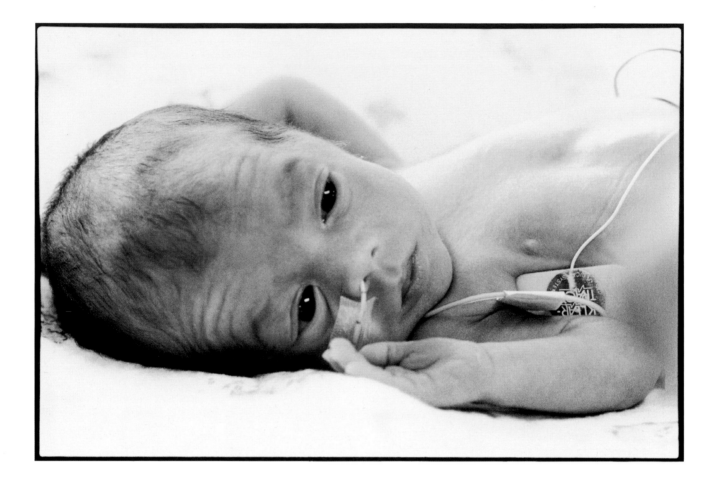

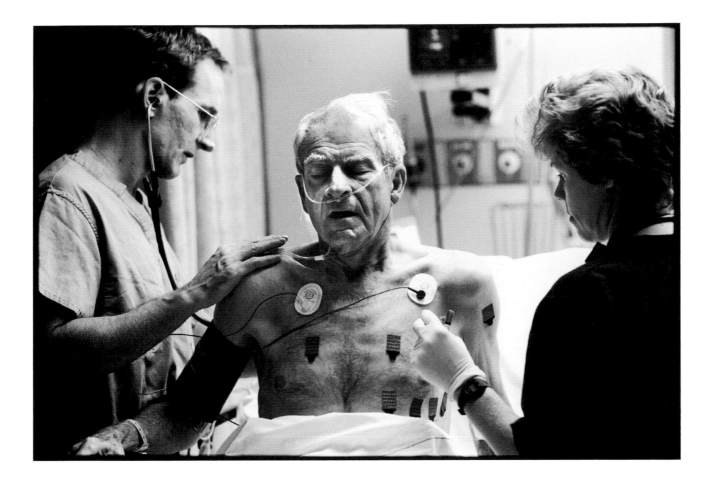

We make a living by what we get.
We make a life by what we give.

Winston Churchill

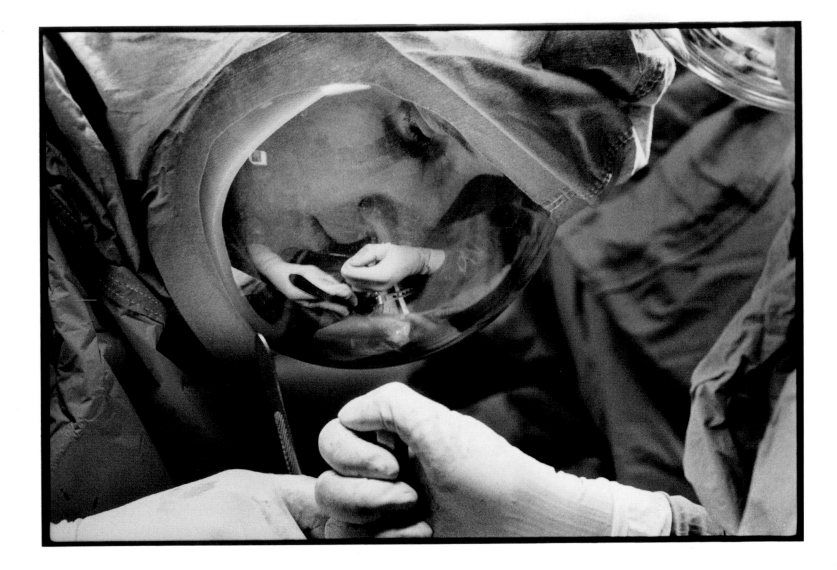

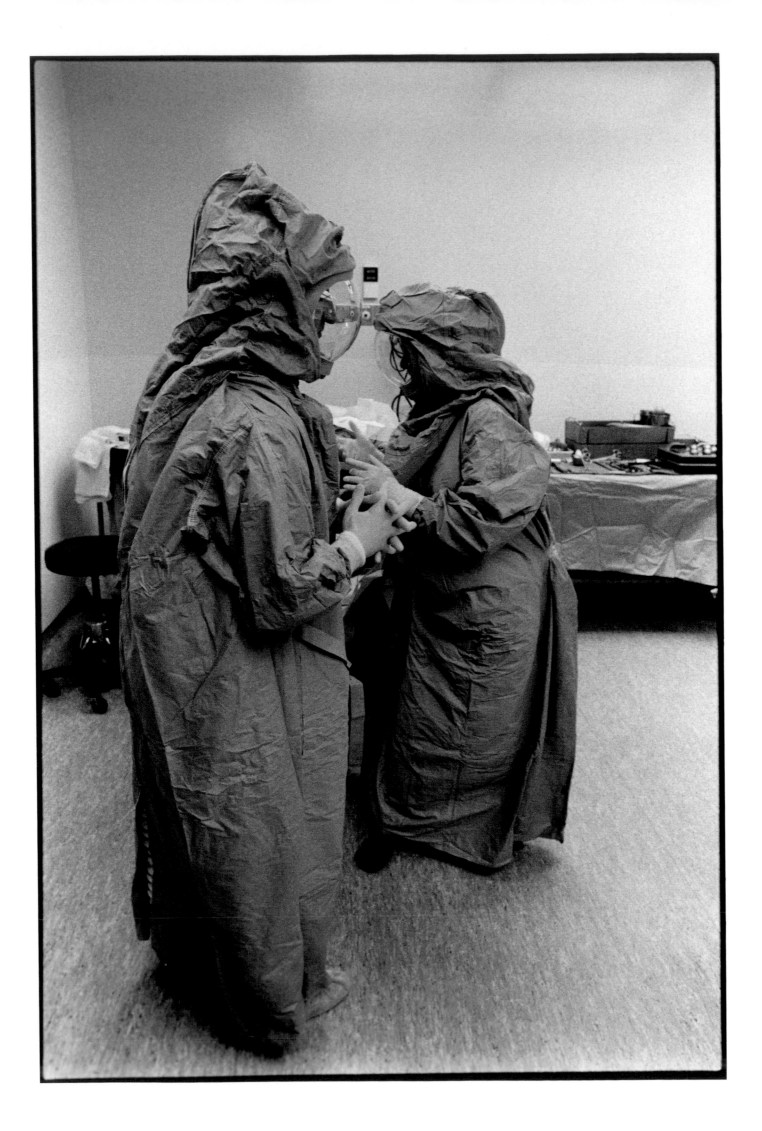

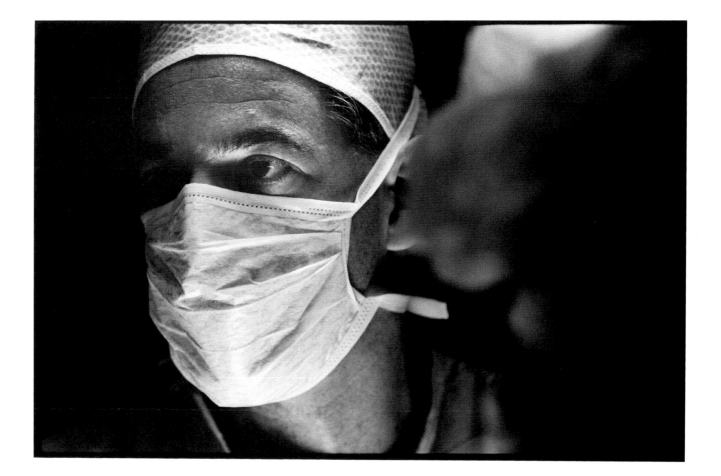

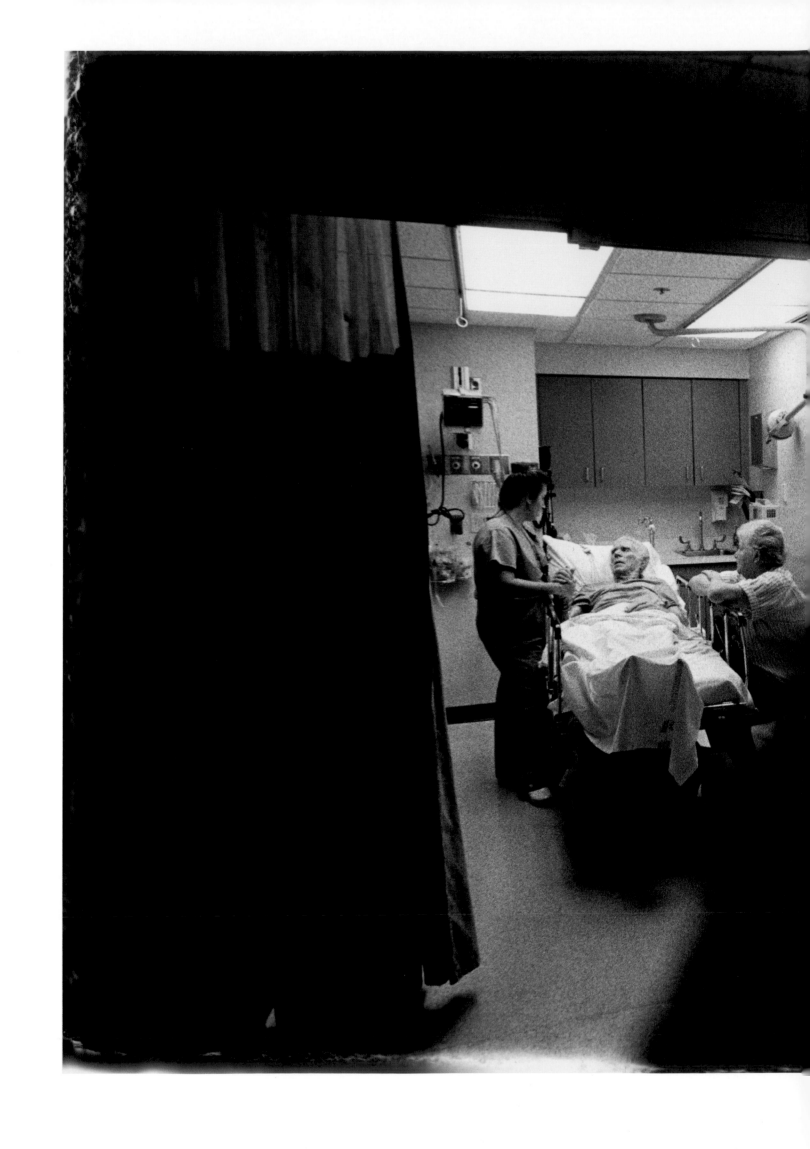

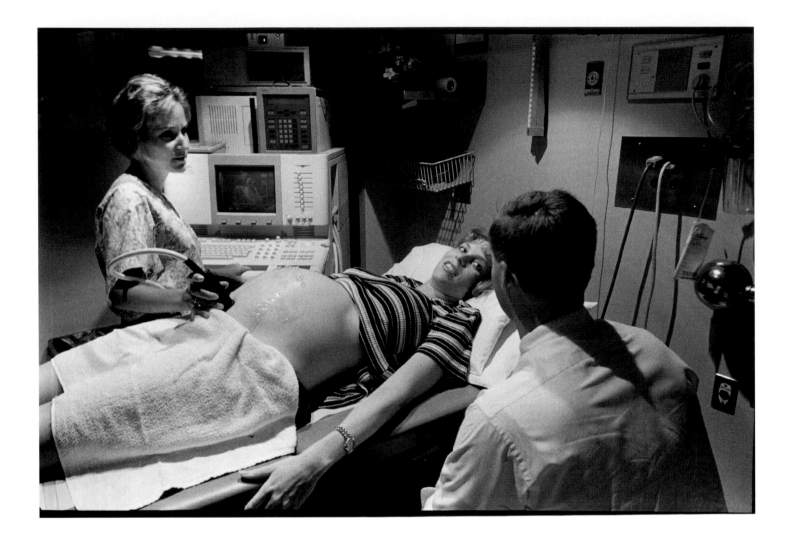

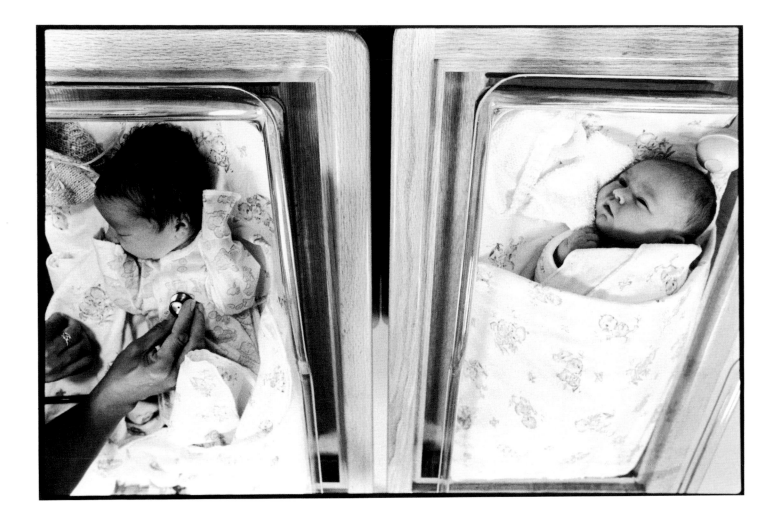

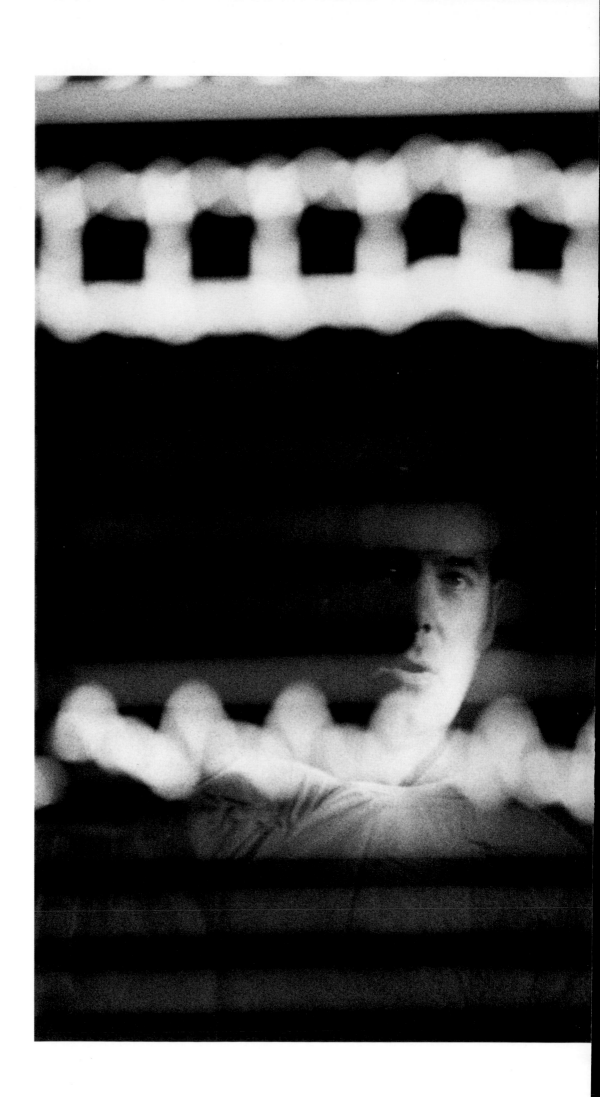

Enthusiasm is nothing more or less than faith in action.

Henry Chester

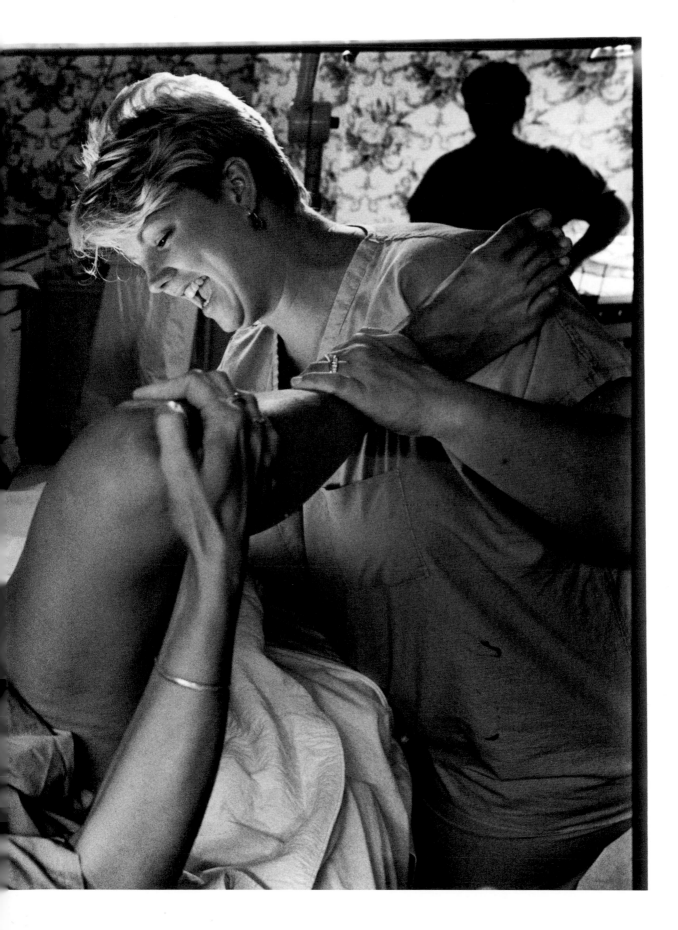

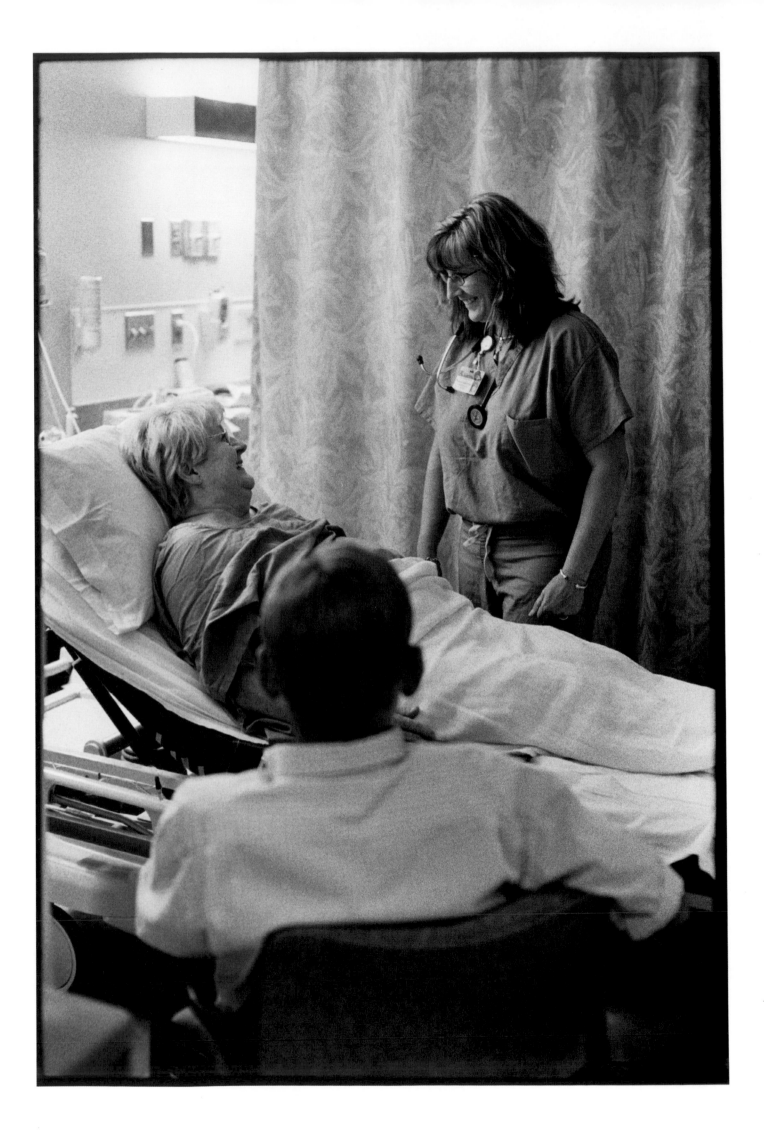

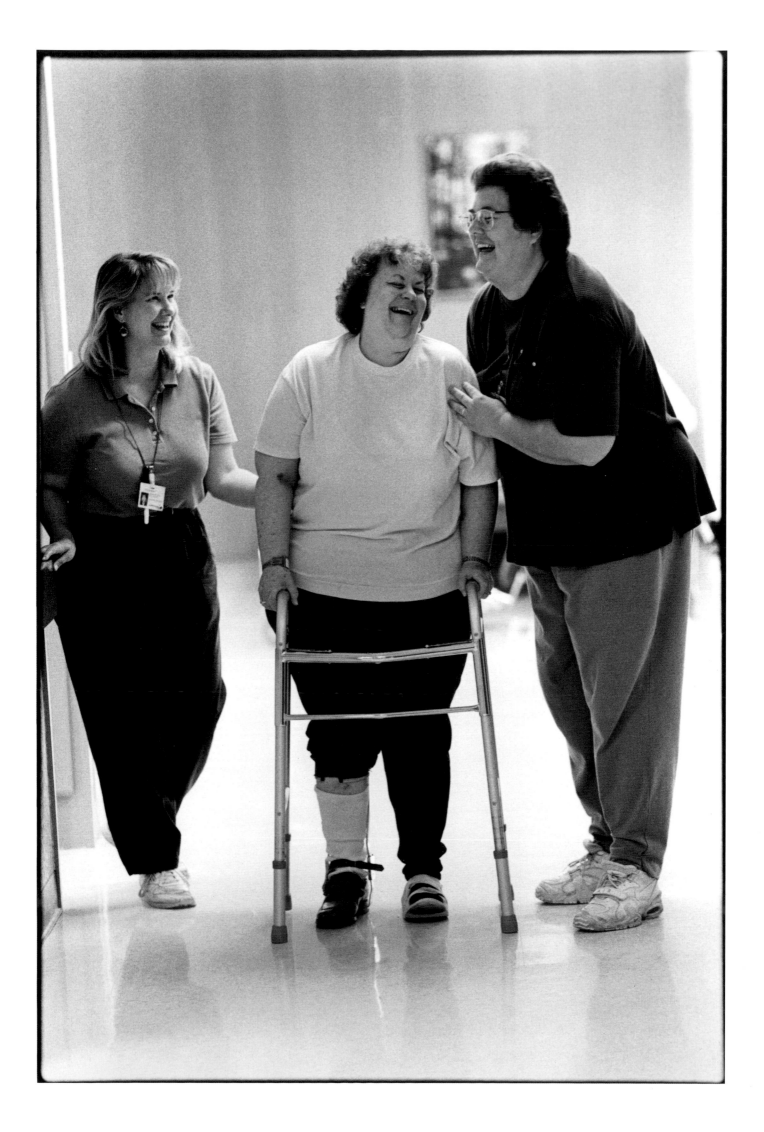

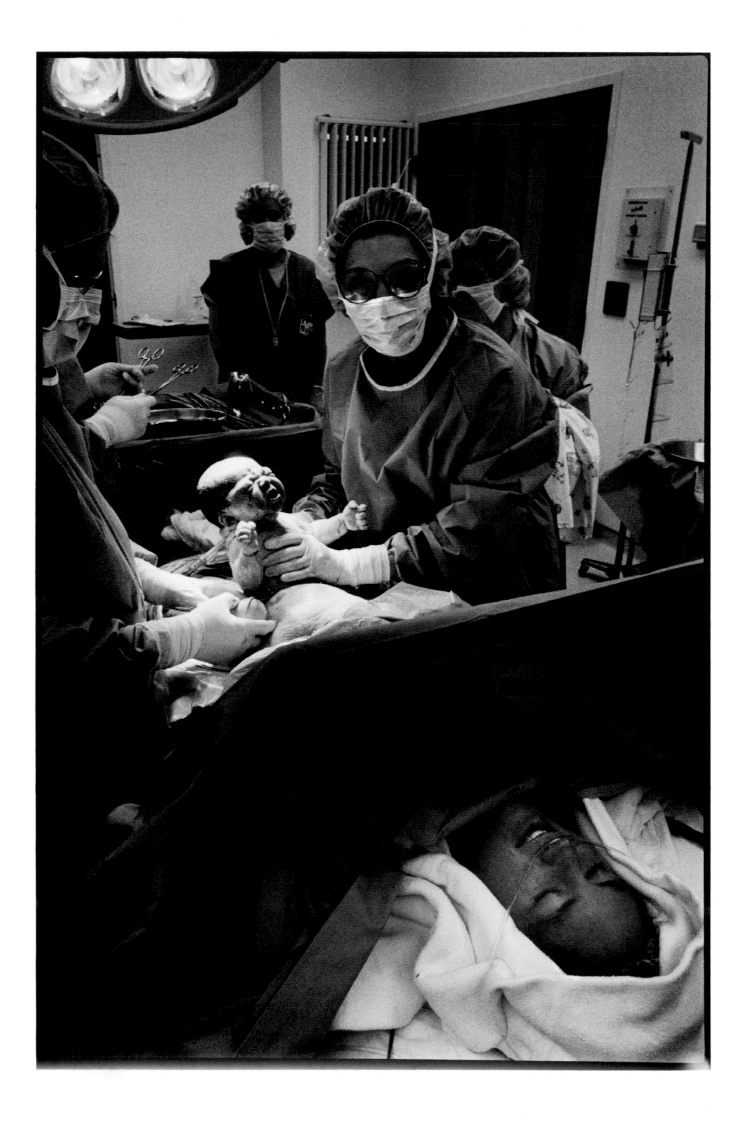

The quality of mercy is not strain'd,
it droppeth as the gentle rain from heaven upon the place beneath:
It blesseth him that gives and him that takes.

William Shakespeare

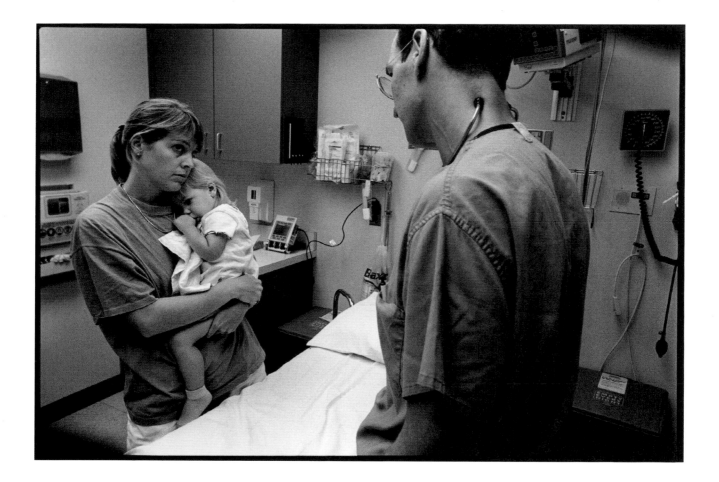

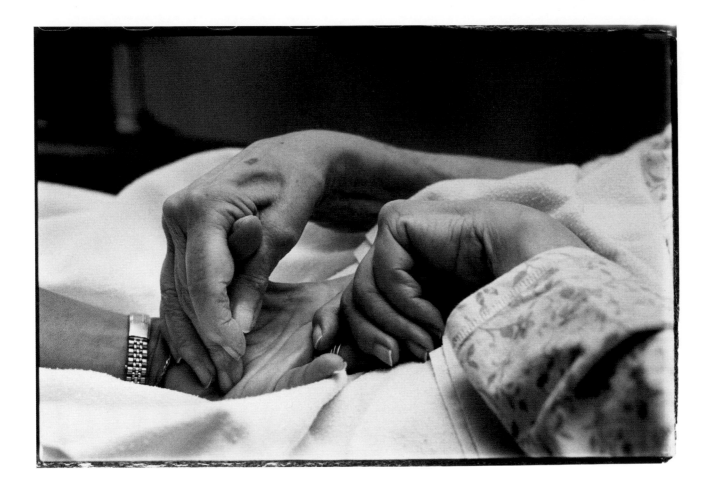

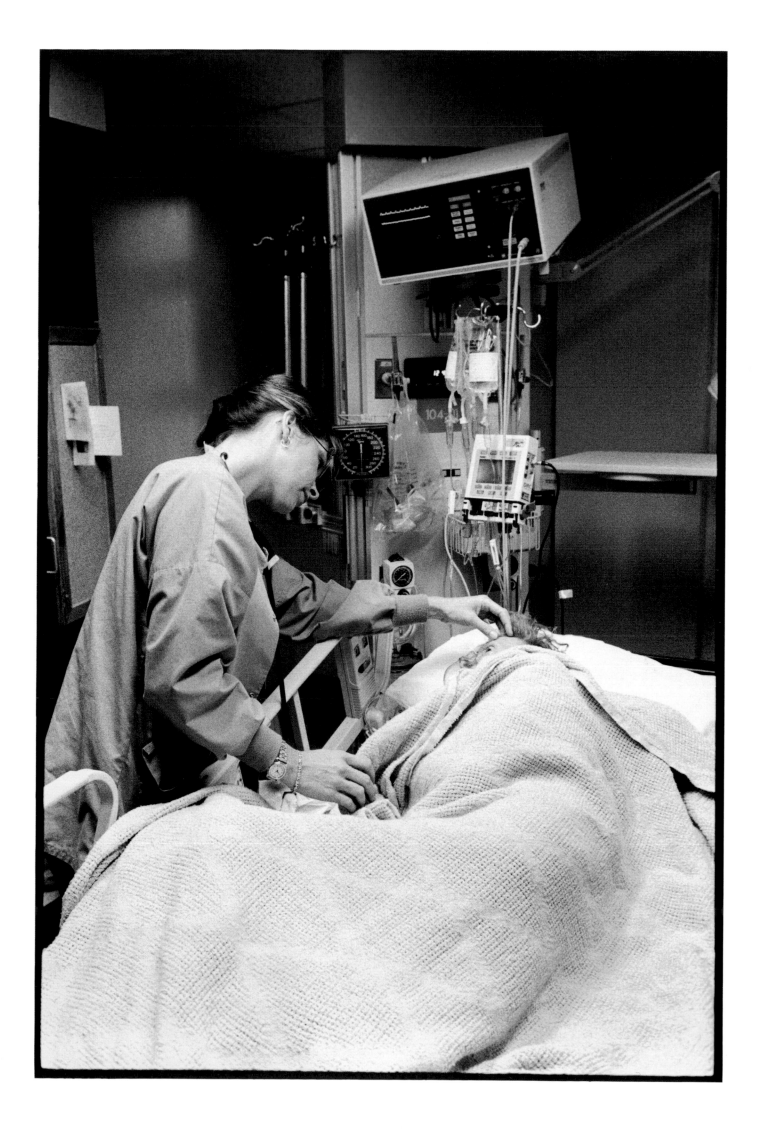

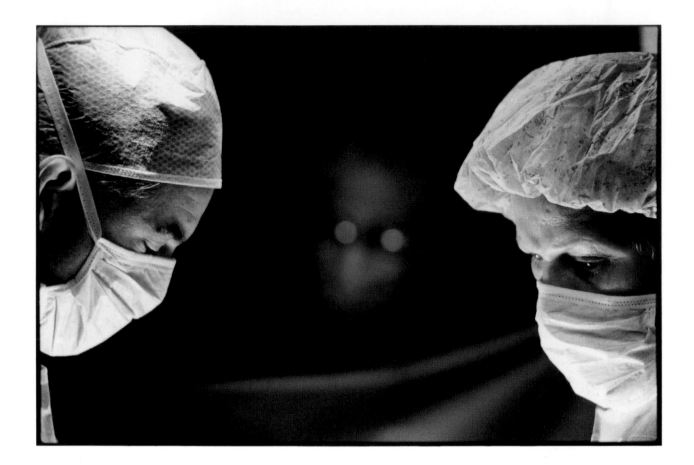

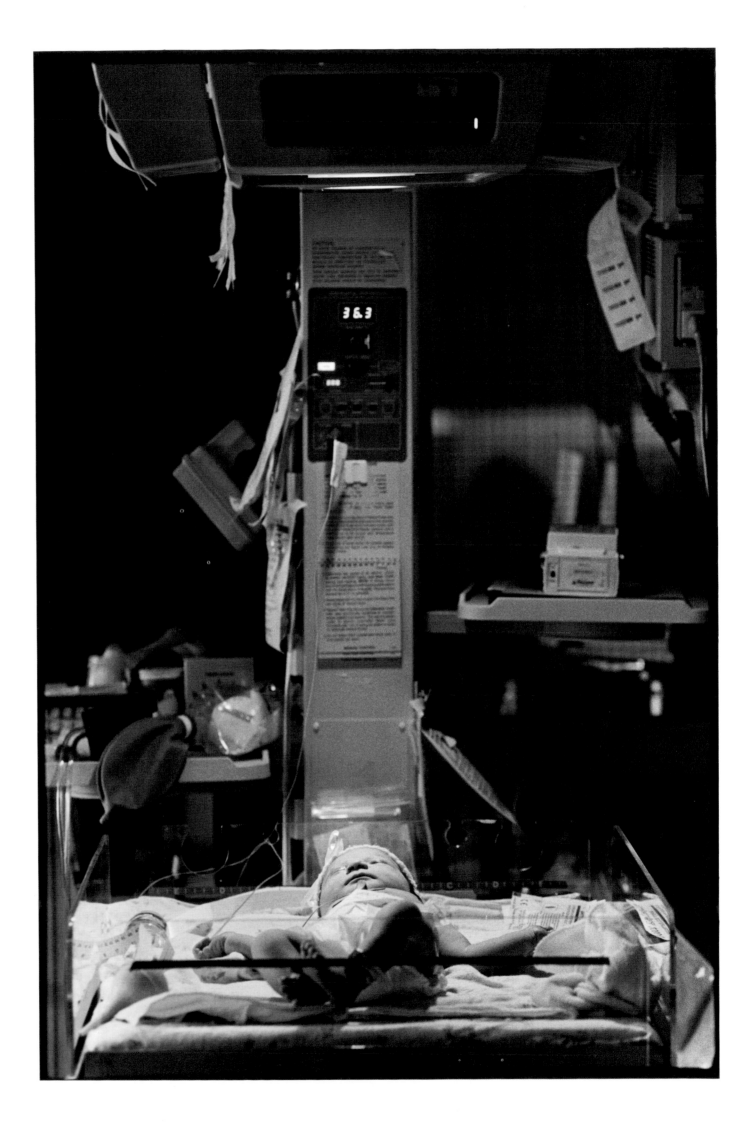

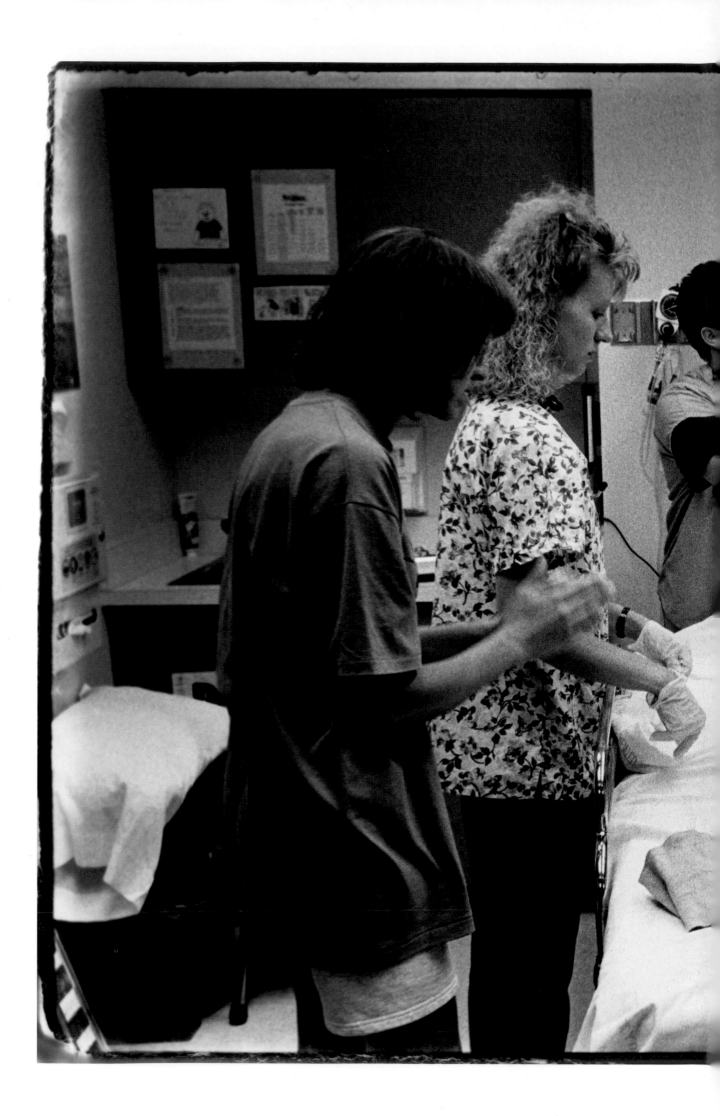

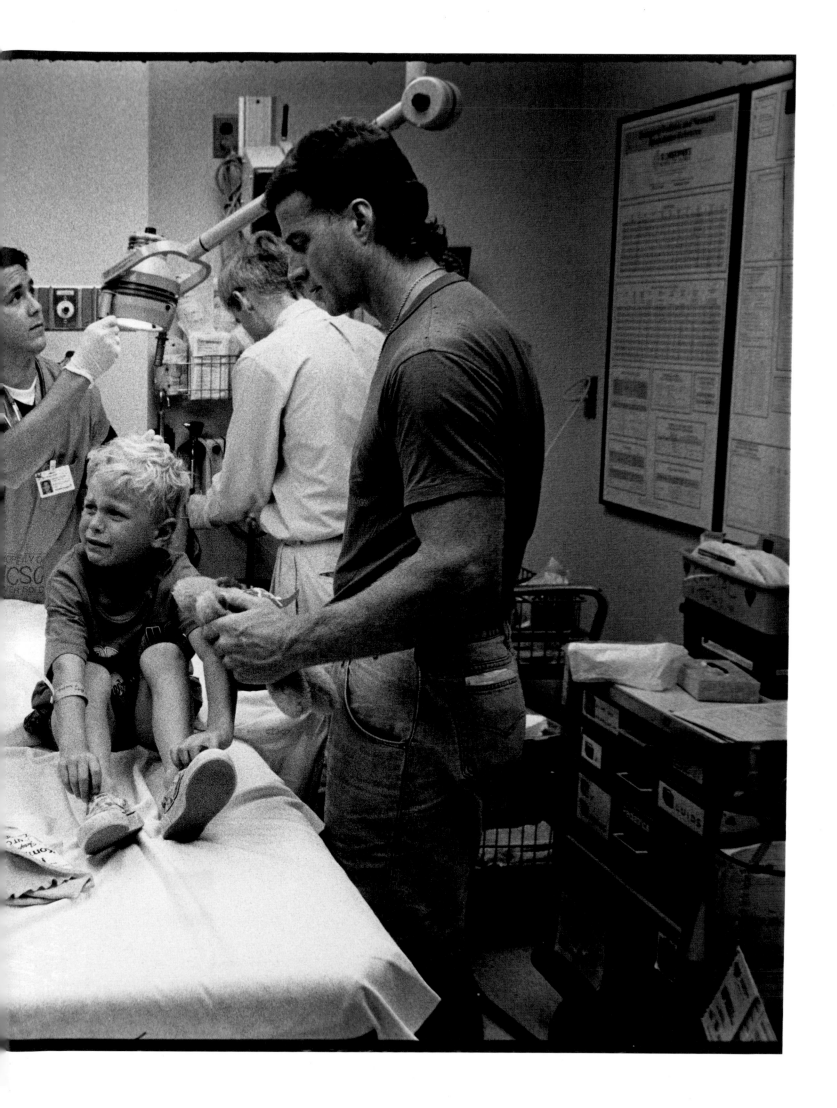

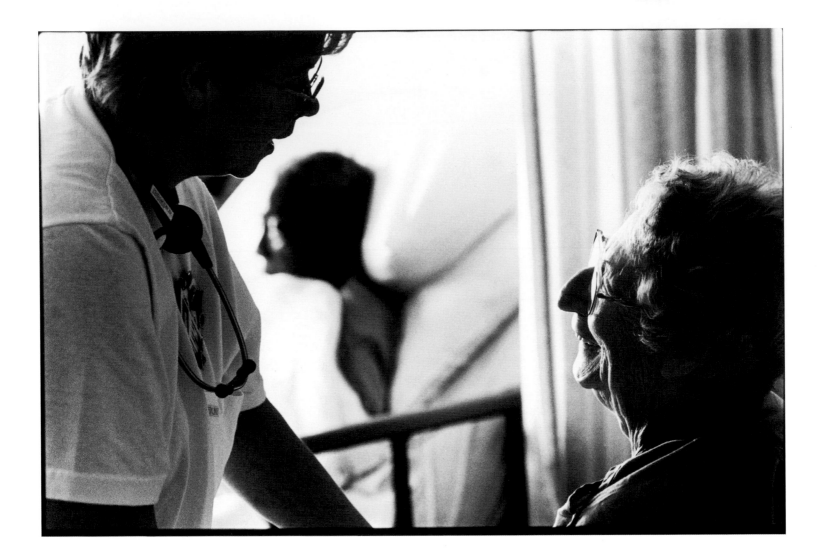

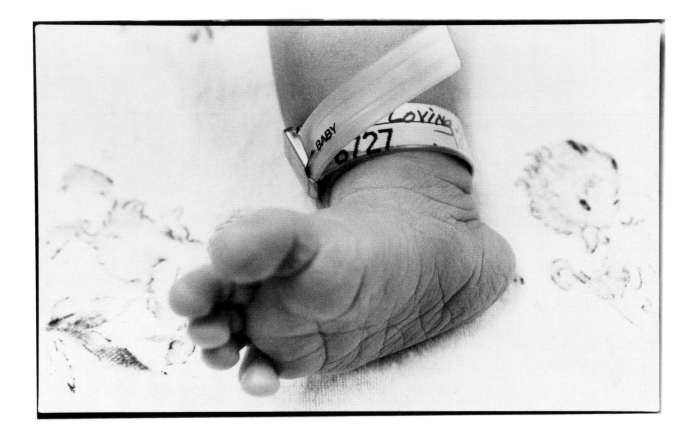

acknowledgements

Special thanks to all members of the Doylestown Hospital family, seen and behind-the-scenes, whose passion for their jobs has made this book possible.

The publication of *Bricks & Mortals* was underwritten through the generosity of an anonymous donor.

THE BRICKS

Doylestown Hospital was founded in 1923 by the Village Improvement Association, a women's club that was established in 1895 to "promote the health and beauty" of the flourishing borough of Doylestown in the heart of Bucks County. Initially intended to provide emergency and maternity care to residents of the largely rural community, the hospital quickly outgrew its original home in a converted Victorian townhouse at Pine Street and Oakland Avenue.

In 1939, Doylestown Hospital moved to a second site: a modern brick building at Belmont Avenue and Spruce Street with 21 patient beds and room to expand—which it did, again and again, until the late '60s. At that point, it became clear that to continue to provide the increasingly advanced and complex medical services the community needed, the hospital would have to relocate once more. Again the leaders of the V.I.A. took up the challenge and helped raise the funds to build the third hospital on a 50-acre campus just outside of town. The current hospital opened in 1975 and has undergone 3 major expansions, the most recent being the addition of The Heart Institute in 2000. As this book is being published in 2008, a new Emergency Department is under construction, to be completed in 2010.

Doylestown Hospital remains a striking building filled with remarkable technology. But the hospital's extraordinary success is based on far more than its architecture and equipment. The heart and soul of Doylestown Hospital are the people who work in it, lead it and believe in it: the doctors, nurses, board members, administrators, technicians, cooks, therapists, housekeepers, secretaries and hundreds of other men and women that provide the human mortar that keeps our building standing tall.